This Is Just to Say

Poems of Apology and Forgiveness

by Joyce Sidman

illustrated by Pamela Zagarenski

HOUGHTON MIFFLIN HARCOURT
Boston   New York

ISBN

978 0544105072

D1496818

Contents

Part 1 APoLogiEs

Part 2 ReSPoNSeS

INTRODUCTION

It is my job to write an introduction to this book. First of all, I am Anthony K., sixth-grader at Florence Scribner School, and this is part of a poetry unit we have completed in Mrs. Merz's class. We liked our "Sorry" poems so much that we decided to put them together into a book. We worked on them and revised them a lot. Then I had the idea of making a second part (which is why I have to write the introduction), where the people we wrote poems to get to write poems in response. So there are two sets of poems in this book, apologies and responses, plus the poem that inspired them all, "This Is Just to Say," by William Carlos Williams (who must have had some interesting nicknames in school). Bao Vang, who is really good at art, took our poems and made the illustrations with the help of Mr. Willow, the art teacher, using her own sketches and some computer art.

I learned a lot from this experience, although I can't say that all my classmates feel the same way. And I can't say all the people writing poems back felt great about it, either. Some of them didn't even do it. So a few of us on the editorial board had to fill in. Because of this book, though, a bad thing that was going to happen didn't. And a mystery was solved. So, at least to us, this is a pretty important book.

We hope you enjoy reading our poems. As Mrs. Merz says, there is a little bit of us in each of them.

Anthony K., Editor

This Is Just to Say

I have eaten
the plums
that were in
the icebox

and which
you were probably
saving
for breakfast

Forgive me
they were delicious
so sweet
and so cold

William Carlos Williams

PART ONE

Apologies

to Mrs. Garcia, in the office

This Is Just to Say

I have stolen
the jelly doughnuts
that were in
the teachers' lounge

and which
you were probably
saving
for teachers

Forgive me
they were delicious
so sweet
and so gloppy

too bad
the powdered sugar
spilled all over my shirt
and gave me
away

by Thomas

to the statue of Florence P. Scribner

Lucky Nose

I am very sorry for assaulting your nose
before every spelling test.

When I first came here
I noticed you right away:
your kind eyes,
your stiff hair rolled in a ball
like my grandmother's.
Your nose looked so strange and magnificent.
I asked Mai Lee about it.
"Pale and smooth
from a thousand rubbings," she said.
Before that first spelling test,
it felt like a cool stone
under my hand, calming me.

In a hundred years
your nose may be worn down to nothing
and so I am very sorry.
But think of all the little children,
again and again,
to whom you gave
that cool stone
of luck.

by Bao Vang

to **Kyle**

I Got Carried Away

Kyle, I'm sorry
for hitting you so hard in dodge ball.
I just really get carried away
in situations like that.
Kids screaming and ducking,
Coach bellowing,
all those red rubber balls
thumping like heartbeats
against the walls and ceiling,
blinking back and forth
like stop lights
(that really mean
go,
    Go,
        GO!)
See,
I even got
carried away
in this poem.

by Reuben

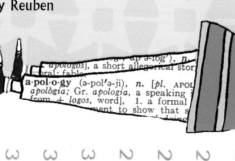

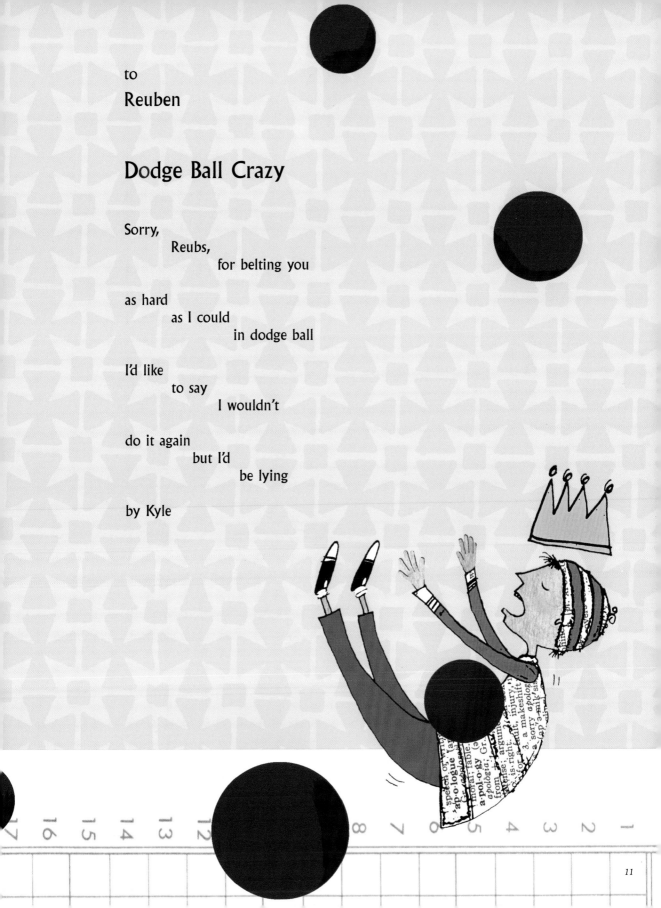

to
Reuben

Dodge Ball Crazy

Sorry,
Reubs,
for belting you

as hard
as I could
in dodge ball

I'd like
to say
I wouldn't

do it again
but I'd
be lying

by Kyle

11

to Mrs. Merz

Fashion Sense

I am so sorry for my rude words.

The classroom was so dead.

No one had anything more to say about *Old Yeller*,

and we were all crazy to get outside.

The silence seemed like a hundred crushing elephants.

So I raised my hand and made that comment

about your dress,

and everyone burst out laughing.

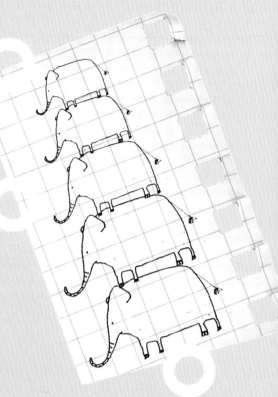

You smiled,

but your smile looked like a frozen pond.

People were high-fiving me on the way

down to lunch, but I felt like a traitor.

You know how the words slip out and you can't believe it?

And they echo in your head forever and ever?

All through lunch, all through recess,

all the next day, I wished I could take those words back.

I kept thinking of what you always say to us:

words can help or hurt, the choice is ours.

I want to rewind to that moment and say instead,

"Mrs. Merz, that dress makes you look like a princess."

You are really a queen, not a princess.

Our queen. *Reina de la clase.*

I hope you will overlook the transgressions

of your loyal but loud-mouthed subject

and forgive me.

(P.S. I notice you're not wearing that dress so much anymore.

Green is not good on you, anyway. I like the new one,

with blue in it, which makes you look thinner.)

by Carmen

Brownies —Oops!

I smelled them from my room:
a wafting wave of chocolate-ness.

I listened for movement,
ears pricked like a bat's.

I crept down, stepped
over the sleeping dog.

I felt the cold linoleum
on my bare toes.

I saw the warm, thick
brick of brownies.

I slashed a huge chunk
right out of the middle.

The gooey hunks of chocolate
winked at me as I gobbled them.

Afterward, the pan gaped
like an accusing eye.

My head said, Oops!
but my stomach said, Heavenly.

by Maria

to my sister
   Carrie

The Black Spot

That black spot on your palm.
It never goes away.
So long ago
I can hardly remember,
I stabbed you with a pencil.
Part of the lead, there,
still inside you.
And inside me, too,
something small and black.
Hidden away.
I don't know what to call it,
the nugget of darkness,
that made me stab you.
It never goes away.

Both marks, still there.
Small black
reminders.

by Alyssa

← sister's HAND

Balance

Dad, I'm sorry for smashing
the garage window when I was a kid.
Felipe and I were messing around
and saw the cracked pane.
One had a crack,
so they should all have a crack, right?
That's what Felipe said.
We hefted some rocks.

Then one pane had a jagged hole.
But they all had to match, right?
Felipe said we should balance them out.
I remember the weight of the gritty rocks,
the shiver of tinkling glass,
the wild joy blooming in my chest,
the fear, the running away.
For a while, it seemed like
the bravest thing I had ever done.

Now I realize Felipe was stupid
to make up a reason to smash things.
And I was even more stupid,
to follow him.

by José

to my mother

Sparkling Deer

Mom, I'm so sorry for breaking

your precious glass deer

all those years ago.

The scent of Christmas was in the air,

and your little snow scene drew me like a magnet.

The deer's slim pink legs

and arching neck:

I could almost feel their smooth, delicate surface.

In my head, I heard you say, "Don't touch!"

but my fingers had a mind of their own.

I plucked it from the rough cotton snow

by its tiny antlers.

Then

it dropped!

Later, when I heard you crying,

I felt small.

Please forgive me.

by Mrs. Ruth Merz

to Maria

Not Really

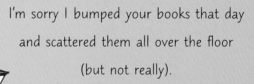

I'm sorry I bumped your books that day
and scattered them all over the floor
(but not really).

I'm sorry your locker mirror disappeared
and mysteriously ended up in my desk
(but not really).

I'm sorry I pulled that clip out of your hair
and you had to chase me down the hall
(but not really).

I'm sorry I made you yell at me
till your face got red and your eyes sparkled
(but not really).

I'm sorry you keep saying
you won't go out with me.
(Really.)

by Bobby

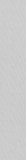

To Manga, My Hamster

I wish I could set you free
like that day you escaped
and ran all over the house.
That was an amazing day.
My mother screamed.
My sister cried.
All because you were loose somewhere,
burrowing through pillows and toys.

When Mom finally found you
huddled in the mop bucket
(and you bit her)
you looked so fierce,
like your wild cousins
that roam the jungles of Asia.
I wish I had jungles to give you.
I wish that could be your life.

Please forgive me.
All I have to offer
is this warm, cozy cage
and my fingers
scratching behind your ears.

    by Ricky

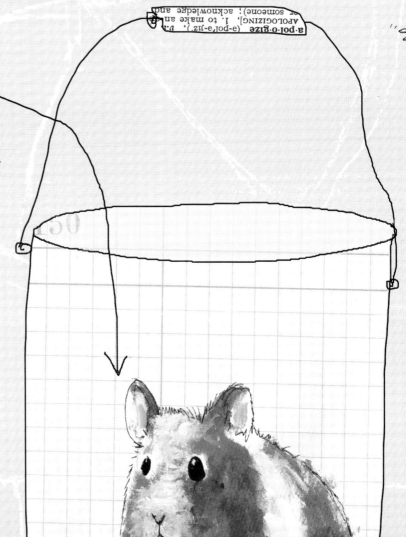

a·pol·o·gize (ə-pŏl′ə-jīz′), *v.i.*
APOLOGIZING). 1. to make an
... someone; acknowledge and

to Einstein, my dog

It Was Quiet

It was quiet. No machines beeped.
You looked like you were sleeping.
Your nose was still wet.
Your ears were still silky.
But inside, something was crumbling.

"It's not sleep. It's a coma," Baba said.
Harsh voice in the quiet room.
"We have a decision to make."
I did not want to decide anything.
I wanted to stay quiet with the feel of your fur.
But inside, all my cells and nerves
were screaming.

Heads nodded.
The decision was made.
You did not move. You did not shudder.
Yet life left you.

I'm so sorry we had to do this.
We wanted to save you some pain.
I hope we did the right thing.

Is death ever right?
I don't know, but I hated having to choose it.
And I hate the quiet in our house
without you.

by Tenzin

to my brother, Lamar

Secret MeSsage

Where would you hide a secret message?
Under a pillow? In a pocket?
Between two slices of bread?
Where would you hide a message
that wants to be found?

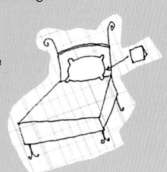

Maybe it shouldn't be found.
Maybe writing it
        is most important.
What happens after
        doesn't matter.

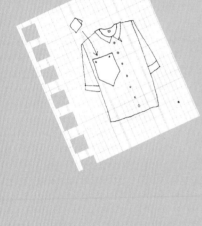

Well, big brother,
here's my secret message:
I'm sorry I'm such a "weird kid."
I'm sorry I embarrass you.

I am hiding it here, under the seat in your car.
I wonder if you will
ever find it.

by DaRon

bee (bē), n.

Spelling Bomb

I can't believe I lost.
I know I disappointed you.
Do you really think I don't care?
I know how important it is to win.

I know I disappointed you;
I saw it in your face when I misspelled.
I know how important it is to win;
I studied hours and hours.

I saw it in your face when I misspelled.
I saw you turn away from me.
Even though I study hours and hours,
I never seem to be your champion.

I saw you turn away from me
and in that moment would have given anything
to be your champion.
To see your bright, triumphant pride.

In this moment, I would give anything—
do you really think I don't care?—
for your bright, triumphant pride,
which I can't believe I lost.

by Anthony

(Author's Note:
This is my favorite poem form, called a pantoum. The second and fourth lines of each stanza are
repeated as the first and third lines in the next stanza. It is also supposed to rhyme, but Mrs. Merz
says rhymes are not as important as meaning.)

to ???????

A Waste of Heart

I'm sorry for loving you
because you never notice me.

I'm sorry I stare at you so much in class,
trying to figure out what's on your mind.

I'm sorry for taking the time
in the morning with my hair,

sorry for trying on six shirts
to find the one that makes you say,

"Hey girl, lookin' fine,"
because you never say it.

I'm sorry
because I know
I'm wasting my heart on you.

Yeah, I'm sorry for loving you.
So sorry that I think I'm going to stop.

by Raneesha

to Bao Vang

What Was I Thinking?

Wow, am I really in the principal's office?
She is bigger than I thought.
Is that gray hair on her neck?
Her dress is the color of ripe plums.
She is asking so many questions!
I have such a bad feeling in my stomach.

    Bao Vang is my best friend.

    She is always laughing.

    She was laughing when she hit the fire alarm.

    It was an accident! She was just fooling around!

The principal's eyes are like hot sparks.
My parents will be so angry.
They will yell and yell.
My mouth is opening!
I'm blabbing about Bao Vang and the fire alarm!
I can't believe this is happening!
The principal sends me away.
I slink out like a whipped dog.

    Bao Vang: my best friend.

    I told on her, then pretended I hadn't.

    Will she ever forgive me?

by Mai Lee

to my
dad

Next Time

You went away and left me.
It's not the first time.

The first time, you left because I cried too much:
    screaming baby, *waah, waah!*
The second time, it was because I messed up at school:
    your daughter is "acting out."
The third time, I came home early and saw . . .
    well, *Forget it,* you told me, so I did.

You see, I'm keeping track.

What did I do this time?
Is it the way I'm dressing these days,
or the way I laugh too loud?
Whatever it is,
I can fix it.

Please, please come back.
Don't leave me spinning alone,
like a slow, sad tornado.

I'm sorry, Daddy.

Next time I'll be
perfect.

by Jewel

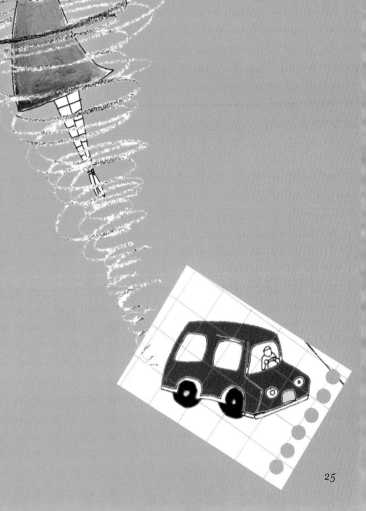

How Slow-Hand Lizard Died

I stole him.

Took him home in my pocket.

Felt the pulse beating

in his soft green neck.

Had no place good to put him.

A shoebox.

He got cold, I think.

Watched his life wink out,

his bright eye turn to mud.

Brought him back,

stiff as an old glove.

Hid him in the bottom of the cage.

Left the money on Mrs. Merz's desk.

(Stole that, too).

Won't touch the new lizard.

Don't like to touch

money

either.

by Anonymous

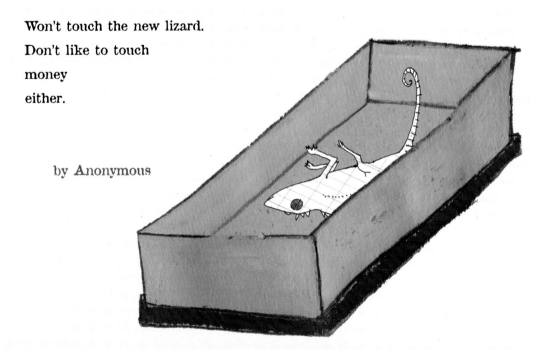

Part 2

RESPONSES

Dear Thomas

Thank you for your poem.
You do have a way with you, Thomas.
Smiling, asking me how I'm doing today,
talking a mile a minute.
Slipping in and out (yes, I see you!)
stealing our hearts, and our doughnuts, too.
A nice boy like you can really
get on in the world
if he doesn't let his fingers run away with him.

Of course I forgive you.
But I still have to call your mother.

by Mrs. Garcia (in the office)

to Bao Vang

To the Girl Who Rubs My Nose

I was a child like you.
I used to run, I used to play.
Now I am old, and cold,
and frozen on my pedestal.
I see a lot from up here:
children
laughing,
crying,
fighting,
holding hands.
I have lots of time to think.
I think maybe spelling
isn't so important.
Friends are important.
Kindness is important.
A gentle touch.

So, come rub my nose again, girl.
come warm me up a little.

by DaRon
(writing for Florence P. Scribner's statue)

(a poem in two voices
by **Kyle** and **Reuben,** for each other)

Dodge Ball Kings

Kyle	Reuben
We're	
Dodge Ball Kings!	*Dodge Ball Kings!*
	We rule the gym!
We like to zing	
	each other.
Dodge Ball Kings!	*Dodge Ball Kings!*
Each ball, we fling	
	with all our might
as though it is our last:	*as though it is our last:*
a catapult,	
	a cherry bomb,
a setting sun,	
	a blazing ring
we fire	
	through air.
We mark each other out—	*We mark each other out—*
zing, bam, sting!	*zing, bam, sting!*
It hurts	
	but we don't care.
We're	
Dodge Ball Kings!	*Dodge Ball Kings!*

to Carmen

Haiku for Carmen

Just these few warm words,
and spring sunlight fills the room;
my dress turns to sky.

by Mrs. Ruth Merz

to Maria

Desk Mess — Oops!

The house was quiet,
so empty and still.

Your door was open,
so I peeked in.

Piles of papers, stacked any which way.
Dust thick as velvet.

My fingers itched to straighten,
clean, organize.

I didn't mean to read anything—
the note from Bobby was an accident.

Afterward, that corner of the room
looked so different from the rest:

an island of neatness
in an ocean of mess.

My conscience said, Oops!
but my eyes said, Heavenly.

by Maria's mom

to Alyssa

Roses Are Red

Roses are red,
violets are blue.
I'm still really
pissed off at you.

by
Carrie (Alyssa's sister)

to José

I'm Telling You Now

Son, I kept telling you
I couldn't write a poem
and you kept saying just
write down a list of how
you feel and break it
into shorter lines like
we do at school
and I kept thinking I
did lousy in school,
every single year almost
and barely made it through and
I never told you about that,
always on you to work harder,
even though I barely tried,
always messing around
like I knew better, but really
just scared because it didn't
come natural for me like
for some, and now here you
are keeping up with the smart kids
and more sometimes and
writing poetry and all and even
getting your old man to write
all these lines, and I want to
say what I'm feeling, which
is I'm proud, real proud
of you, I couldn't be prouder
and somehow I've written
this poem if you could
call it that and christ
forget about the window
it's ancient history.

by José's dad

to Mrs. Merz

For Little Ruth

Why are you sorry, my little Ruth?
The deer is perched happily on its crust of snow.
It cannot leap anymore
but it is happy, almost as happy
as the day it was made: I watched
with big eyes as it grew in the glassblower's
hands like a piece of crystal taffy.

You were a boisterous child. I cried
the day I got your poem. Not because
I was sorry, or because you should be sorry,
or any of that. No, no. I cried because
you were little, and now you are not.
Come visit me soon, will you?

by Mrs. Merz's mother

to Bobby

What Girls Want

Girls want a lion with a great shaggy mane.
Girls want a horse, fast and sure.
Girls want a coyote that sings with its heart.
Girls want an eagle, soaring through mountains.
Girls want a breeze that whispers its name.
Girls want a snowfall that makes the world new.
Girls want a dog that wags all over.
Girls want a cat that purrs to the moon.
Girls want a hedgehog that carries its own armor
      but doesn't
      always
      use it.

Just to let you know.

by Maria

Sorry Back, from the Hamster

I'm sorry I bit your mom's finger
and hung on to it like that.
Hamsters are not normally
bloodthirsty,
but I'd had a lot of adventures by then
and I was tired.
Her hand was a huge scary claw
coming at me.
The blood tasted like rust.

The truth is, at first
I was so, so happy to be free!!!
But later I was so, so glad
to be back
curled in the warm palm
of your hand.

by Ricky
(writing for his hamster)

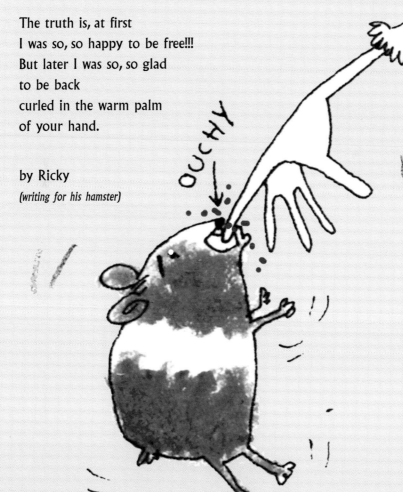

37

Losing Einstein

I had to do the same with my Sasha, not long ago.
No one can tell you what it's like, until it happens.
No one can see those trusting eyes.

Dogs are different from us, they don't think so much.
They just feel like crazy.
They love you if you treat them right,
and fear you if you don't.
They can handle pain, but they hate being left behind
when they're old or sick.
They want to be right there with you.

Einstein was right there with you, Tenzin.
Even if his eyes weren't open,
he was smelling you, feeling your touch.
You were loving him, and he was loving you back.
That's how he went.
And that's how a dog should go.

by Mr. Johnson (custodian)

to DaRon

Little Brother

Little brother,
you are one weird kid. Hiding stuff under my seat.
Why you got to hide? Life should be lived Extra-Large.
Look at me, man. I am living large as I can.
I know when I got to stand, and when I got to run.
But I been thinking about you, little bro,
since you put that note in my car.
You got your own stuff—stuff I don't have.
You got sticky shoes. They stay on the ground.
You got brains that work ALL the time, not just some time.
You got that curly hair of Momma's. You don't remember, but I do.
You got that smile, that dumb sweet smile that ain't seen badness yet.
Keep all that stuff. Keep it. Hold tight to it.
Hold it, little brother, hear? You gonna need all that stuff.
Maybe not the smile—get rid of that
or you'll end up on the street under somebody's wheel.
But the other stuff. Don't let it get beat out of you.
Stay strong. I'll be showing you, anyways.
Showing you how to live large,
Extra-Large, like me.

by Lamar (DaRon's brother)

(Editor's Note: DaRon changed a few words in his brother's poem so we could print it.)

to Anthony

Some Reasons Why

Why must we work so hard,
and always be the best?

Parents say:
  hard work builds character.
I say:
  too much hard work means no laughter.

Parents say:
  only the best get ahead.
I say:
  everyone's good at something.

Parents say:
  daydreaming is just an excuse for laziness.
I say:
  they just never learned how to write a poem.

  by Tenzin

  (writing for Anthony's mother, who said he was being ridiculous)

to Raneesha

Dark-Haired Girl

Raneesha
dark-haired girl
with flashing eyes

Raneesha
long legs pounding
down the track

Raneesha
frown that breaks rocks
laugh that starts tidal waves

Raneesha
strong
      fierce
           loyal

Our Raneesha
don't change
      who you are

by Carmen & Mrs. Ruth Merz

to Mai Lee

The River of Forgiveness

Here I am,
reading Mai Lee's poem.
I am wading into the river of forgiveness.
Thinking of alarm bells,
of breaking glass, of confusion,
and the fear that crushes your heart
when you've done something wrong.
I feel cold and alone, fighting
the water as it pulls at me and fills my eyes.
Will I ever make it across?
I keep thinking of a friend
who helped explain the world,
whose arm is always around my shoulder,
a friend who stands with me in the crowd.
There she is—my friend,
on the other side of the river.
She's the one looking worried
when I cough and choke,
the one about to jump in after me.
But wait—my feet are touching!
I've reached the sandy bank!

I've crossed the river of forgiveness.
I open my arms to her.

by Bao Vang

My Poem

Daddy wrote back.
He was late, but he wrote.
He was late, he was sick,
he was almost gone for good,
but he wrote to me.
"Dear Baby," he said,
"You are perfect.
So perfect.
It's me who's not.
None of the stupid things
I have ever done
are even close to being your fault."

He says he was at the end of his rope one night.
Then he saw my handwriting
on an envelope and it called to him.
He says he was going to leave this world
and my poem called him back.

He says my poem saved his life.

He says he is coming back,
really coming back to stay
if he can, and the first thing
he wants me to do
is teach him how to write poems like that.

That's what Daddy says.
And this time
I think I believe him.

by Jewel

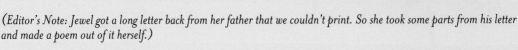

(Editor's Note: Jewel got a long letter back from her father that we couldn't print. So she took some parts from his letter and made a poem out of it herself.)

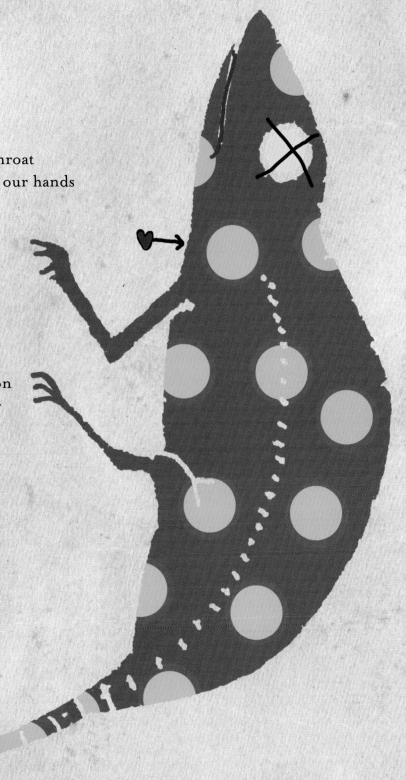

'to Anonymous

Ode to Slow-Hand

the way his heart beat in his throat
the way his toes whispered on our hands

los perdonamos

his skin: rough green cloth
the color of new leaves

los perdonamos

his belly: soft as an old balloon
his tongue: lightning's flicker

los perdonamos

the sad way he left us
the sad way you feel

los perdonamos
we forgive you

by Mrs. Merz's class

The Library of Congress has cataloged the hardcover edition as follows:
Sidman, Joyce.
This is just to say: poems of apology and forgiveness/by Joyce Sidman;
illustrated by Pamela Zagarenski.
p.cm.
I. Apologizing—Juvenile poetry. 2. Children's poetry—American.
I. Zagarenski, Pamela, ill. II. Title.
PS3569.I295T47 2007
811'.54—dc22
2006009820

ISBN: 978-0-618-61680-0 hardcover
ISBN: 978-0-544-10507-2 paperback

Manufactured in China
SCP 10 9 8 7 6 5 4 3

4500536704

*T*o all my students—*past, present, and future*—

who allow me into their hearts.

*A*nd special thanks to the esteemed poet and teacher

Kenneth Koch, whose book Rose, Where Did You Get

That Red? *pioneered the use of "poetry ideas," and whose*

New York City students wrote the first "Sorry" poems.

—*J.S.*

For my niece Abigail

—*P.Z.*